In Hiding
Animals Under Cover

Written by Melissa Blackwell Burke

STECK-VAUGHN
ELEMENTARY · SECONDARY · ADULT · LIBRARY

A Harcourt Classroom Education Company

www.steck-vaughn.com

Animals in nature often need to hide themselves.
They have amazing ways to make sure they aren't seen.

An animal's colors can help it blend in with surroundings.
This is called camouflage.

Some animals hide so they can hunt easily.

Their camouflage helps by making them hard to see.

Other animals hide so they cannot be hunted easily.
Their camouflage helps by making them hard to see.

In the forest, the bobcat blends in with rocks.

It leaps out to catch the animal it hunts.

In the rain forest, the chameleon changes colors.
It uses camouflage to surprise the tiny animals it hunts.

In the sea, an octopus can change colors quickly.
It changes colors so other animals will not see it.

The leaf insect's shape and color make it look like a leaf.
A bird looking for an insect to eat may pass it by.

Doesn't the sea dragon look like seaweed?

This animal tricks the fish that want to eat it.

Most birds fly away from danger.

The woodcock uses its colors to hide.

In snowy places, some animals change colors.

The arctic fox is brown in summer but white in winter.

The snowshoe hare is brown in summer.

It changes to white in winter to hide in snow.

In the desert, the rattlesnake uses its color to hide.

It looks just like desert sand.

On the side of a tree, a moth sits very still.

The colors of its wings look like tree bark.

What animals might be hiding near your home?

Look closely in the grass, leaves, and trees.